CONTENTS

KU-471-056

CHAPTER ONE
THE ACADEMY AWARDS..... 4

CHAPTER TWO
GROWING UP 8

CHAPTER THREE
WORKING WITH HOLLYWOOD DREAMS........ 14

CHAPTER FOUR
SUPERSTAR 20

Glossary 28
Timeline 29
Activity 30
Find out more 32
Index................................. 32

CHAPTER 1

THE ACADEMY
Awards

Lupita Nyong'o stood on stage. She wore a long blue dress. She held a golden trophy.

She looked out at the crowd. Everyone was standing. They clapped and cheered for her.

BRIGHT
IDEA
BOOKS

LUPITA
Nyong'o

by Stephanie Watson

raintree

a Capstone company — publishers for children

Raintree is an imprint of Capstone Global Library Limited, a company incorporated in England and Wales having its registered office at 264 Banbury Road, Oxford, OX2 7DY – Registered company number: 6695582

www.raintree.co.uk
myorders@raintree.co.uk

Text © Capstone Global Library Limited 2021
The moral rights of the proprietor have been asserted.

Edited by Charly Haley
Designed by Laura Graphenteen
Original illustrations © Capstone Global Library Limited 2021
Production by Colleen McLaren
Originated by Capstone Global Library Ltd

978 1 4747 9380 3

British Library Cataloguing in Publication Data
A full catalogue record for this book is available from the British Library.

Acknowledgements
We would like to thank the following for permission to reproduce photographs: AP Images: Dave Bedrosian/Geisler-Fotopress/picture-alliance/dpa, cover, Matt Sayles/Invision, 6–7; Rex Features: Jaap Buitendijk/Focus Features/Kobal, 15, Marion Curtis/Starpix, 10, Moviestore, 21, Warner Bros/Kobal, 13; Shutterstock Images: Debby Wong, 16, Dfree, 27, Featureflash Photo Agency, 24–25, Jaguar PS, 5, Kathy Hutchins, 19, 22, 28, Sopotnicki, 9, wavebreakmedia, 31
Design Elements: Shutterstock Images

Printed and bound in India

It was the 2014 Academy Awards. She had won an award. It was for her first film **role**. She played the character Patsey in *12 Years a Slave*.

Lupita Nyong'o showed off her Academy Award.

She spoke to the crowd. She thanked other people who had worked on the film. She thanked her family.

Then she had a message
for children around the world.
She said their dreams matter.
She cried as she spoke.
Everyone cheered again.

Nyong'o spoke to the
crowd at the 2014
Academy Awards.

CHAPTER 2

GROWING
Up

Nyong'o was born in Mexico City in 1983. Her parents are from Kenya in Africa. They moved back there after she was born. She grew up in Nairobi in Kenya. She has five brothers and sisters.

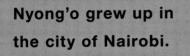

Nyong'o grew up in the city of Nairobi.

KENYAN CONNECTIONS

Nyong'o has family in the Luo **tribe** in Kenya. Former US president Barack Obama also has family from this tribe.

Nyong'o has always loved acting.

10

ACTING

Nyong'o went to an all girls school. She loved acting. She performed skits at family parties.

She auditioned for a play when she was 14 years old. It was *Romeo and Juliet.* It was at a small theatre. She got the lead role of Juliet.

Nyong'o wanted to be a famous actor. She liked watching American television. But she rarely saw women with dark skin like hers in films. She prayed for lighter skin.

Then she saw *The Color Purple*. The women in the film had dark skin. She saw she could be like them. She could be a famous actor too.

Whoopi Goldberg in
The Color Purple

CHAPTER 3

WORKING WITH Hollywood Dreams

Nyong'o moved to the United States in 2003. She went to college to study film.

She worked on a film during one of her summer breaks. The film was called *The Constant Gardener*. It was filmed near her home in Nairobi. She did not act. She helped behind the scenes.

A scene from *The Constant Gardener*, starring Rachel Weisz and Ralph Fiennes

Nyong'o has worked on many different film projects.

Nyong'o moved back to Nairobi after college. She got her first big acting role in 2009. She starred in the TV series *Shuga*. It was shown on MTV in Africa.

That same year she made a film called *In My Genes*. It was about people with **albinism**. They have no colour in their skin and hair. The film showed how badly these people were treated in Kenya.

Nyong'o wanted to be a better actor. She moved back to the United States. She went to Yale University.

She graduated in 2012. She got the role in *12 Years a Slave* that same year.

Nyong'o has become very famous in the United States.

19

CHAPTER 4

SUPERSTAR

12 Years a Slave made Nyong'o a star. She once feared her dark skin would stop her from acting. Now she was famous. She had even won an **Oscar**.

Nyong'o in
12 Years a Slave

Nyong'o is now famous for more than acting.

Nyong'o also became a model. She modelled for a famous make-up company. She has been in adverts and magazines.

MOST BEAUTIFUL

People magazine named Nyong'o its "Most Beautiful" person in 2014.

STARRING ROLES

Nyong'o got many roles after *12 Years a Slave*. She played Maz Kanata in a Star Wars film. She was the voice of the wolf Raksha in *The Jungle Book*. She played Nakia in *Black Panther*.

Nyong'o (third from left) and the stars of *Black Panther*

She got a star on the Hollywood Walk of Fame in 2019. She was 36 years old.

HELPING OTHERS

Nyong'o uses her fame to help others. She supports groups that help animals.

She also supports other black women. She speaks out about how black women are often treated badly. For one magazine photo shoot she wore her hair in a ponytail. The magazine erased her ponytail in the photo. She was angry that the magazine changed her hair. She believes women do not need to change to be beautiful.

Nyong'o speaks out for what she believes in.

GLOSSARY

albinism
condition in which a person is born without colour in their skin and hair

Oscar
famous award given to someone who works in film, also called an Academy Award

role
part in a TV series, film or play

tribe
group of people, often with a similar background, who usually live in the same area and have a leader

TIMELINE

1983: Lupita Nyong'o is born in Mexico City, Mexico, on 1 March.

2003: Nyong'o moves to the United States.

2009: Nyong'o writes and directs the film *In My Genes*.

2009–2012: Nyong'o stars in the MTV series *Shuga*.

2014: Nyong'o wins an Oscar for *12 Years a Slave* on 2 March.

2019: Nyong'o gets a star on the Hollywood Walk of Fame.

ACTIVITY

MAKE A COLLAGE

Create a collage of people you admire. You can cut out their photos from magazines, or you can print out their photos from the internet. While deciding who to include in your collage, you can ask questions such as:

- What are their careers?

- Why do they inspire you?

- What good have they done in the world?

- How are they similar to or different from each other?

FIND OUT MORE

Books

25 Women Who Dared to Go (Daring Women), Allison Lassieur (Raintree, 2019)

National Theatre: All About Theatre, National Theatre (Walker Books, 2017)

Sulwe, Lupita Nyong'o (Puffin, 2019)

You Can Work in Movies (You Can Work in the Arts), Samantha S. Bell (Raintree, 2019)

Websites

www.marvel.com/movies/black-panther
Visit the Black Panther official website.

https://wonderopolis.org/wonder/can-anyone-be-an-actor
Find out what it takes to be an actor.

INDEX

12 Years a Slave 5, 18, 20, 24

acting 5, 11–12, 17–18, 20, 24

albinism 17

Black Panther 24

films 5–6, 12, 15, 17, 24

Hollywood Walk of Fame 25

magazines 23, 26

modelling 23

Nairobi, Kenya 8, 15, 17

Yale University 18